INTO THE DISTANCE

ROXIE BERRY

ISBN: 979-8-9902680-2-9

Publishing By: DemiCo National, LLC

www.DemiCoNational.com

Art

Hey, have you noticed lately that you have been the million- dollar art piece that made every room you have ever been in ten times better? When looking at art, you will notice that every piece is not the same. From the colors, strokes of the brush, scenery and even the picture frame! Just like yourself; you have a different skin tone, walk, lips and even tone of voice but you are still a masterpiece. Your presence will always light up the room you are in because you yourself are a million-dollar work of art. You have encountered a Calligraphist that calls you wonderful, confident, chosen, talented and powerful but do you believe it? Remember what was said earlier that you are the art piece that every room needs to make it beautiful.

Trust

Do you trust people more than you trust yourself? If your answer was yes, why is that? Has anyone made you feel that you are inadequate to lead yourself in deciding for yourself? Make the decision today to trust yourself with every excellent choice you make. No, you do not need the validation of man to make the step just do it out of faith. There will be times that trusting yourself becomes uncomfortable but knowing that your trust is really in the one bigger than you it will be easier to take that step. I challenge you to decide for yourself this week and reflect on the difference you felt from others making your decision rather than yourself.

Keep Fighting

Man, life sure does suck at times! Not having enough for your own needs, robbing Peter to pay Paul, working to make ends meet or even failing to live up to your own standards. I tell you this do not count the days but make the days count. Even if adversity makes the best of your life, better will come but you cannot give up. How will you see better if you give up now? Take the same towel you are about to throw in and wipe your sweat off and keep going. If life were easy everyone would rejoice about it but how can you build endurance without going through hardship? Life is not meant to break you but to strengthen you, use your life as an example of how a winner looks. Life is just a bowl of sour patch kids it is sour than sweet.

Awake

Awake

Breathe in and out yes, you are alive.

That smile of yours is a life changer.

That voice of yours echoes with joy from room to room.

The courage that you have will stand tall before you.

Awake

Live everyday like it is your last.

Not counting the days be sure to make them count.

Fight through the barriers and you will see the result.

Awake from your slumber and see who you really are.

Why?

Why?

Everything must be a lesson.

Why?

Am I not enough?

Why?

Did I become friends with you?

Why?

Didn't I keep my distance?

Why?

Didn't I let go when I had the chance?

Why?

Do I have to be the one to figure it out?

Why?

Am I not perfect?

Why?

Sometimes, I cannot find the answer to my own questions.

Why?

are you asking why instead of being confident that you are

just the way you are for a reason. No one can be like you because you are the best version of yourself. Instead of asking why, embrace the current and move forward.

Free

Free

From Being miserable from past mistakes.

Free

From being held captive in your mind from negative thoughts.

Free

To walk away from things that do not mean any good to you. Free

From The chaos because it is not necessary.

Free

To Do what brings you joy without the embarrassment.

Free

To find your way and give your circumstances and situation the best version of you.

Free

To be yourself. Your worth is priceless.

Free

To give yourself grace and mercy. Free like birds who spread their wings and fly.

Free

Does not cost much, it is free! Just be happy with your accomplishments big and small.

Greener grass

The saying goes that the grass is not green on the other side. What happens when that grass becomes green one day? The seeds that you have planted throughout the years have been watered which then makes the grass grow healthier. Stop looking into other people's yard and focus on watering your lawn. Everyone has a dry patch but for it to become healthier, you have to water it and as you water it, the grass will become green, stay focused on your lawn, and watch every seed that you have planted sprouts in a matter of months. It will become greener watch and see.

Demeanor

I give off a strong demeanor, but Life became overwhelming. I separated myself from all my family, friends, school, and work to practice this strong personality that was not me at all. The anger, frustration, screams, and nightmares all due to the tragedy have caused me to become numb. How could I pour anything healthy in somebody else when everything becomes unhealthy in my life? "I have to be the strong one" I tell myself every day. The positive aspect of life became a doorway to something negative. I gave myself the inch to feel the pain, but I must be the strong one, so I quickly snapped out of it. To the one reading this, it is ok to not be a strong person all the time! Take time to feel your emotions and deal with them.

Into The Distance

As a young girl born and raised in Bessemer Alabama, she saw her world through the eyes of love and compassion until it was all gone in a short second. Her world shattered where justice did not prevail. She hid the love and compassion Buried in her spirit and soul where it would never become exposed again. How could she go on with life as if it were normal again? Would she ever be able to see the world through the eyes of compassion and love again? Little did she know there was love deep in the distance that was wrapped up in the little heartbeat that she would hear three years later.

Living in it

Take a moment to reflect, do you see it? Do you see that you're standing in the atmosphere that you spoke about two years ago? Do you see that you're standing in the atmosphere that you dreamed about? The path and the road getting here was hell and high waters, but you've made it. You pushed through the sweat and the tears and you've made it. Now you can laugh about it and say to yourself, "that wasn't as hard as I thought it would've been." But don't get comfortable because you have more road ahead of you. Continue to speak it into existence and pressing forward you will see the fruit of your labor.

Agape love

The love that never runs out The love that extends beyond emotions The love that man cannot give without God.

The love that is pure

The sacrificial love

Agape love is loving me beyond my flaws.

This type of love is the love that everyone needs because this love will keep you warm inside and does not waver. The love that does not hold a grudge. The love that is not rude or boastful The love that forgives.

This type of love is the love that everyone needs because this love will keep you warm inside and does not waver.

Agape love

I will Reap What I Sow

The garden that grew in my life was the product of the seeds I planted. I tried to plant good seeds so that in return my garden would reflect pureness, purpose, prosperity, passion, and pleasure. We all know that no one would like the seeds that they have planted to grow to be rotten. Being mindful of the seeds you plant will determine what type of plants will grow in your garden. Treat people how you want to be treated and the same will happen towards you. Give to those in need and people will give to you. Watch what you do and say because you cannot escape the consequences of one's actions. You will have to work daily so that your garden will produce good fruit! How does your garden look? Is your garden filled with weeds or filled with beautiful plants that grew from love?

Pretend

I cannot pretend l like you.

I cannot pretend I want to have a future with you.

I cannot pretend to make myself happy being with you.

I cannot pretend I am in love when I am not.

I cannot pretend I am going to give you the world when I do not have one to give.

I cannot pretend to be more than something that I am not. I cannot pretend to live in your fantasy world when there is nothing to gain.

I cannot pretend anymore. That would hurt me to my soul dearly.

I cannot pretend to be something that I am not.

I cannot pretend to say you will have the best life with me. I cannot pretend to be the best thing you ever had in your life.

I cannot pretend to love you when there is nothing to love. I cannot pretend to be the woman you always want and desire.

What I can do is enjoy who I was born to be Roxie Berry.

Happy

H: here is to hope and a future.

A: applying everything that I have been taught while,

P: planning the next steps for my future. P: patiently waiting to hear the words Y: You have made it now take your rest!

Fill in the blanks.

I am _____ and I can _____. If I could be anything in this world, I would be a _____. In order for me to become a _____ I have to _____. I am_____, _____ and _____. One thing that has happened in my life that has made me stronger was _____. I may not have liked what happened, but I am still here. I _____ (insert your name) vow to put my best _____ forward in everything that I do. I will become everything that I desire to be, and it will not be long from now.

It is okay to cry!

Let it out! Scream if you must but do not hold it in. The tears you cry and speaking the words your mouth could not. I pray that the tears you cry today will not be the tears you cry tomorrow. We are created to feel our emotions and sometimes we feel them through crying and that is okay! When you cry help will be sent and the comforter will clothe you in peace and help you along the way. If you have ever been told that crying is a sign of weakness well, I come to disrupt that teaching and tell you that way a lie. Let it out! Scream if you must but do not hold it in!

Absent Presence

I miss your presence, and I miss your smile and I even miss the way that you held me in the midnight hour. It would be easier for me to get over you if we had never met! There is a song that says, "you can't miss something that you never had" and sometimes I wish I never met you. It is pointless for me to fight for you because you never will fight for me. I will always love you, but I must move on, what I thought was love was just me filling the void of my abandonment issues.

Spiritual love

I know when you are close because I can smell you before you enter the room. "You're so beautiful and you smell so sweet" those are the words you whispered to me! You know how to make love to me with your words and it makes me tingle with a sensation I cannot explain. OMG!

OH MY GOSH! The smell you left behind has me thinking of the next time we will see each other. Will it be like this again or will he try something new? I am on the edge of my seat!

Nighttime Love

Whenever I have a dreadful day, you reassure me that my day is going to get better. You are the sponge that soaks up my pain and you make me a better person. Before I go to bed, we talk about our issues before going into the next day. We never went a day without saying I love you and/or I forgive you because that made everything better. You know me better than I know myself, when I start a sentence you could finish it if you wanted to because you know me so well. You would pray for me and then we would pray together! Without you there would not be a me.

Good Day

I am about to have a good day!

I will command my day and speak victory!

I am about to have a good day!

I will not allow the attitudes of the next person to destroy my day!

I am about to have a good day!

I have breath in my lungs, so I have another opportunity to right my wrongs! I am about to have a good day!

Through sunshine, rain, sickness, and pain I will have a good day!

I choose to see the days differently instead of complaining I will see the good! I am about to have a good day!

Who are you?

Are you the one who sits alone for lunch? Are you the one who wears baggy clothes because that is when you are most comfortable?

Are you the one who changes their hairstyle every two weeks?

Are you the one who works 12 hour shifts and then comes home and does schoolwork?

Are you the one who imagines themselves performing in front of an audience when cleaning?

Are you the one who cries when they are upset?

Who are you?

Are you the one who gives their all to those you love?

Are you the one who forgets your own needs? Are you the one who fights back tears when people are hurting? If you have said yes to one of these, I want you to remember that all of this makes up who you are and that is okay! You are perfect just the way you were created.

Mix match!

Your words are sweet like honey but sting like a bee. I do not know if I should believe you or take every word that you give with a grain of salt. Some days you are kind and the next you are mean, why is that? Did I do anything to push you over the edge? It is like walking on eggshells; I have to be incredibly careful not to crack a shell because I do not want to be in the line of fire when you are upset. You have shown me who you are, but I did not want to believe it because I knew who you could be. I know now that I need to believe people when they show me who they are for the first time. No longer will I accept the way that you have been treating me because I know this is what I do not deserve. Let your words match your actions and then I may believe you better.

Pressure

The pressure that you are feeling is not a terrible thing! Yes, I know that it can become too much but the result will be magnificent. While going through the season of pressure remember what you are being taught that way when you have another issue like this you can overcome it. Pressure promotes growth and growth promotes willingness. Be willing to go through the pressure so that you will have the willingness to become better. It will take work, but it is all worth it. Remember the plants that you sow will be the product of your garden so plant seeds to endurance, power, and humility. Pressure promotes growth and growth promotes willingness. The pressure that you are feeling is not a terrible thing! Yes, I know that it can become too much but the result will be magnificent.

Undervalued

You are valued and you are loved! Just because they treated you as if your value did not matter does not mean you are not valuable. Do not forget your worth and do not accept less than. If he/she/ or they cannot respect you then move on! Make the long story short because they heard you the first time-Ziyadah Jackson if they cared about your values, they would not cross your boundaries so do yourself a favor and move on. You are not undervalued they just do not know how to accept all of you and that is okay! You are valued and you should remember that.

Your perspective

If I were to show you a picture of a cup that was half full, how would you describe it? Some would say the glass is half full and others would say the glass is half empty. Neither answers would be wrong but based off your perception is how you would describe a thing. Just because I do not see something the way you see something does not mean your view is wrong. Different perceptions make up a multimillionaire company and that is what I want you to think about when you perceive a thing. Say to yourself the way I perceive a thing does not mean I am wrong and my view of it can expand their way of thinking. Put your thoughts out there and watch how helpful they really are!

Your perception matters.

Breakfast in bed

Wake up breakfast is ready! The notably smell of bacon hit my nose as soon as I woke up! You thought enough of me to meet me for breakfast, and I cannot thank you enough. It is not so much about breakfast but the care that you have for me to make sure I have what I need. If I could I would give you the world and breakfast in bed every morning. The hearty grits with cheese showed the love you out in the food while cooking it. Thank you for breakfast in bed because it shows me the love and care you have for me. If I could I would give you the world!

What will it be?

My eyes became wide when our worlds almost collided together. We tried to set time aside to become better for one another, but it did not work. The stride that we put in was not enough and that was a bummer. I would hope that there was a different outcome, but fate said differently. Looking back over this we were nearsighted only seeing what was in front of us and not what was to come. Could we have made it work? Could he have looked beyond my flaws and I beyond his? Man, oh man what a task this would have been and my question to you "are you willing to work through this no matter how hard it gets?"

Good Character You are brave.

You are careful.

You are charming.

You are captivating.

You are bold.

You are charismatic.

You are assertive.

You are attentive.

You are approachable.

You are compassionate.

You are determined. You are fearless.

You are enthusiastic.

You are logical.

You are optimistic.

You are refined.

You are well-mannered.

You are a person of good character!

Power

That power inside of you helps you go when you are tired. That power inside of you shows you where to go and how to get there.

That power inside of you will help you keep your temper to a low medium.

That power inside of you will take you where your feet cannot.

That power inside of you helps you fight the silent battles in your heart.

That power inside of you was in you since birth.

That power inside of you gives you strength. That power inside of you is so great that when you walk by people they are moved. That power inside of you

Conquer

Poetry is rare, interesting, and different. Just like our love! We do not love the same as others do and that is what makes our love unique. We may fight then make up after a few minutes and others may fight and make up after a few hours. Poetry is rare, different, and interesting just like the words you have spoken to me. Poetry is rare, interesting, and different just like the way you protect me from harm seen and unseen.

Me VS. Me

The battle is self vs. self! Trying to decide whether to do right or wrong. Trying to figure out how to respond, should I respond in anger or with love? Trying to figure out if you look better in long pants or short pants, trying to figure out if you are more confident when quiet or being outspoken. Trying to figure out how to win the battle between self vs. self will have you fighting for your life. I tell you this FIGHT AND DO WHAT IT BEST FOR YOU! The battle between self can be hard but you know what is best for you so do that.

The battle between self vs self is no joke.

The Golden Hour

My life has become better than I thought it would be and yours will too you just have to keep living. My life may not have been sunflowers and rainbows but even through the rain I made the best of it. I did not just leave for me, but I lived for those who I loved and wanted to see make it. This is the peek of something great and I will keep living to see the golden hour. Have you seen the golden hour in your life yet? Have you experienced better yet? Have you always seen rain, or have you seen sunshine too? Keep living and you will see that life is worth fighting for.

Unanimous

The two have now become one in agreement to do life together. Yes, we have our own desires but will die to our flesh for the best of one another. Being of one mind you will sacrifice a lot! What have you sacrificed to get the job done? It is not about you, but it is about the need and wellbeing of the other. We may not agree completely, but we will come to a conclusion that includes the feelings of both parties involved. When you are faced with an issue next time think about how your spouse, friend or family would react and make a wise decision. You can be in agreement with two different outlooks on the issue.

My morning suns.

I watch as you sleep at sunset.

I watch how you brush your teeth.

I watch how you tie your shoes.

I watch how you listen when someone is talking.

I watch how you respond.

I watch how you walk with your head high.

I watch how you prepare your food for work.

I watch how you care for others.

I watch you because you are captivating and a sight to see! I will forever watch you and enjoy the moments of being with you.

Spontaneous

Just do it!

Buy the new house, just do it!

Buy the new car, just do it!

Take him/her on a date, just do it!

Cut your hair, just do it!

Start a book club, just do it!

Everything does not have to be planned out, what if the plans go wrong?

Sometimes life is better when you are being spontaneous. Are you spontaneous or a realist? I challenge you today to do something spontaneous and watch how deciding it will make you feel. Live free because you will only live on this earth once! Have something to look back on and say that was fun I am glad I just did it!

Romance

The romance you desire starts within. Love yourself so that you are a living example to people in which will show them how to love you. Have you loved yourself lately? What does that look like to you? Romance is the feeling of excitement that you get associated with love. Showing excitement to yourself through love can be taking yourself on a date, getting your hair done, taking a me day to rest and even going for a walk. Love you and others will know how to love you! The romance you desire starts within.

Honeymoon

Now that the wedding bells are silent, and the smoke has cleared, what is next? It is time to work; work together on how we will do life together as a team. We will learn how to manage petty disagreements. We will tackle the problem and not each other! What will we do now that the witnesses are gone? We will enjoy the honeymoon while also planning the future. The honeymoon phase does not have to end here but it can be a recurring chapter. Our life will continue to be long and happy. The honeymoon is for us to get to know each other on a level that we have never experienced and that will be us throughout life. We will always learn about one another deeper than the time before.

Wedding Bells

Do you hear that? It is the wedding bells singing a song of commitment. Today is the day that I choose you in front of many witnesses. Today is the day that we make a vow! I will vow to love you, I will vow to care for you, I will vow to speak life into you, and I will vow to be with you until death separates us! I chose you because you first chose me. I am nothing without you because you complete me! I am the bride, and you are the groom. The groom sacrifices and protects and the bride is submitted to you. I will forever follow your lead and trust that you are leading me in the right direction! Do you hear that? It is the wedding bells singing the song of commitment. I WILL FOREVER CHOOSE YOU!

Read Me!

Hey, I hope you have enjoyed the poetry so far! I hope that you were able to relate to some, if not all the poems on a level that encourages you to keep going and becoming better. I am proud of you for noticing where you are now and being content. Better is coming but now is good. Keep going and putting your best foot forward. Roxie Berry

www.ingramcontent.com/pod-product-compliance
Lightning Source LLC
Chambersburg PA
CBHW060357130626
46553CB00003B/1267